Guabancex

CELIA A SORHAINDO

PAPILLOTE PRESS
London and Trafalgar, Dominica

First published in Great Britain by Papillote Press in 2020
23 Rozel Road, London SW4 0EY, and Trafalgar, Dominica
www.papillotepress.co.uk

© Celia A Sorhaindo 2020

The moral right of Celia A Sorhaindo to be identified as the author of this work has been asserted by her in accordance with the Copyright, Designs and Patents Act, 1988. All rights reserved. No part of this publication may be reproduced, stored in a retrieval system or transmitted in any form or by any means, electronic or mechanical, including photocopying, recording or any information storage or retrieval system without the prior permission of the copyright owner.
A CIP record of this title is available from the British Library

ISBN: 978-1-9997768-7-9
Design by Andy Dark
Printed and bound by Y Lolfa, Talybont, Ceredigion, SY24 5HE
Cover photograph: satellite image of hurricane Maria heading for Dominica on Monday, 18 September 2017 (NOAA/RAMMB).

Acknowledgements

With thanks and gratitude to:
My dear family, tt, The Nature Island Literary Festival (NILF) organising team, chaired by Dr. Alwin Bully and Dr. Schuyler Esprit (also Create Caribbean founder and director) and all who contributed and performed over the years, Polly Pattullo of Papillote Press, Vladimir Lucien, Oonya Kempadoo, Dr. Kimone Joseph (Head, The University of the West Indies (UWI) Open Campus Dominica), Dominica Division of Culture, faculty and staff of the Department of Literary, Cultural and Communication Studies, The UWI St Augustine Campus, Trinidad and Tobago, including Dr. Maarit Forde and Dr. Muli Amaye, Vievee Francis and Gregory Pardlo (The Callaloo Creative Writing Workshop) and the CCWW Chapel Hill 2017 cohort, Merle Hodge, Funso Aiyejina, Danielle Lyndersay (The Cropper Foundation Caribbean Writers programme), the Cropper 2016 Balandra group and all the writers who visited, *The Caribbean Writer* and *Moko* magazine families.

Many thanks also to the editors of the following publications where versions of these poems first appeared:
Invoked – *Susumba's Book Bag* – guest editor Shivanee N Ramlochan
In The Air – *Interviewing The Caribbean* journal – Dr. Opal Palmer Adisa

For the Ancestors, Mum (Alexandra), Dad (Martin), siblings (Kenneth, Carol, Michael, Auraum Benneurt), husband Paul and Waitukubuli Warriors past, present and future; your love and support nurtures, guides, grounds and holds me together in infinite ways.

This collection is named in recognition of the ancient indigenous peoples of the Caribbean. One of these groups, the Taino, named the supreme female spiritual entity associated with all natural destructive forces, Guabancex.

– CONTENTS –

a poem filled with words not metaphors – 1

Hypotonic – 2

In The Air – 3

Ajai Alai – 6

Thank You – 7

Myrmecology – 8

Mudras – 10

Ode For Mum's Missing Roofing Screws
(Somewhere Still In The Universe) – 11

Horology - TimeXemiT(ion) – 13

Invoked – 14

H2.5AZ (Strong Ties, Galvanized) – 18

Metamorphosis – 19

Housing Revolution – 20

My Sister & I Are Picking Mangoes – 21

What Do I Know – 22

Hurricane PraXis (Xorcising Maria Xperience) – 24

a poem filled with words not metaphors

im not going to sit here and paint a heavy hurricane picture for you to
visualise in pretty clever metaphor words will never carry you to what
its like actually lets just leave it like that words cannot ever take you
there at all although to be fair Mum is always saying kannót is a boat
all word is metaphor
this will never be real
in a billion years i dont
want some reader to come here think
this world of words was literal think
this blank ink represents black feeling
or that this white page feels any thing
this is what the hurricane left me with
go out and experience it for your self
metaphor the world however you want

Hypotonic

not one of us understood
how the water got into the
sealed places that she did;
the unopened containers—
shut drawers, the basement,
the closed-up vessels—we
cried and cried for months—
even now writing, I well up.

In The Air

After the hurricane,
my grandmother,
in her basement storeroom,
hunkered down,
knelt
her knees raw with prayer
the whole long long lashing tail of night, then
ascended slippery stairs
hoping by holy intervention
her home had been saved.
She stared from room to room,
swaying like a punched drunk spirit,
mouth and eyes wide black holes of disbelief,
words gone as wounds appeared.
She walked on water,
treading over eighty years of floating debris,
then could do no more than silently thank
her saviour over and over for sparing her life.

After the hurricane,
after Mass,
tales of rampant looting
circled among them like hungry dogs;
after the turned-inside-out but still well
clothed congregation, still
silent, had shared signs of peace.
No one appeared to conjure and divide
loaves and fishes between some people;
divided by good and bad luck or circumstance;
divided by ability or will to pad and prepare,

concrete seal, pantry stock, insure against calamity.
But having enough or not enough saved,
surely meant little then,
after all none were saved
from that almighty
hurricane that reined in our poor
island and had everyone drowning.

After the hurricane,
came the crazed lines for food...
for any kind of fuel;
came the tell-tail spoors
of rats and roaches tracking rubbish;
dank despair
threading desperation through the dark.
At night my grandmother floated
in and out of light, nightmare-laden, sleep,
waiting for the chain rattle
of locked door;
for the bark signalling predators
had come for what little she had left.
She prayed for enough strength and grace
to give the strangers what they came to take.

After the hurricane,
she said sometimes it felt
like man eat man survival,
every woman for herself.
Who had time, air, breath, breadth enough,
to free dive deep and long enough,
to understand
then these heads heaped,
backs breaking,

carrying stolen mud-crusted sofas, sinks,
spirits,
through debris to homes
miraculously still standing?
To understand then the tragic
improvised or organised
bacchanal trashing of schools and stores?
Who could explain anything then?
Understand or explain anything now!

When she was able,
my grandmother told me
about after the hurricane.

Months later I flew home
and stood stone still
in the ruin of her home,
alone.
I thought
fear
faith,
had been uncovered,
illuminated, as I watched
a mass of untethered particles
air-floating in the beam of
my head
lamp, from floor all the way above
my head
to the star spored heavens.

Ajai Alai

I thought we had seriously prepared for this hurricane;
bought the supplies, bagged the important, boarded-up
openings, but as I sit bare foot, sore, soaked, shocked, in
rising pool of water, bony back pushing against bulging
wooden walls, I realise I have been impressively naive
again about the boundaries beyond boxed imagination;
the surreal reality which can actually be birthed—a whole
nation of unforeseen…revelation. This, this, bulging-wall
force, squeezing water through thread-vein cracks in wood,
breaking out, breaking in, breaking us—is unimaginable.
I shout, hand gesture my husband, let us leave the wall,
save ourselves, run for cover down stairs to concrete
bathroom. But he has invested so much of his life into
all of this; bits of him strewn in and out of our home, it
is more than his life is worth to stop trying to save it now.
There are endless loud cracks, crashes—I see myself
lifted, flung, flying across the room, landing head first
into bookshelves; imagine this hysterical poetic ending.
I do not know what time is doing but decide to stay here
with him and push and push against this wall, until…
Years ago, I had abandoned prayers of Catholic parents
and searched for my own resonating words, and lately
have been trying out mantras for their sound and effect.
So now I push and push, chant and chant, over and over.
Ajai Alai…Aganjae Alaykhae, Ajai Alai…Aganjae Alaykhae;
Invincible Indestructible…Unconquerable Indescribable.
The unimaginable beating down in time time time with me…

Thank You
After W.S. Merwin

Listen—
In exhausted dawn silence, damp rising mist, we are
thinking—thank you. We are waking, counting our
dead, weighing up damage, picking slow way through
glass, seeking water, finding food, and thinking, thank you.
We do not look at the sky, the windows are gone, standing
in water we look down, then out, and think thank you—still.

There is no news, no current and the phones have no charge.
The cars are not where we left them, the roads, bridges and
safety rails are gone, but we go on thinking thank you. Police
are armed but not beating our doors; they are not home, not
at the station, but guarding the stores—thank you, we think.
Past and future do not yet exist and we think, thank you.

We do not hear birds but see forest blown down, rivers rage.
Our faces dead, drained, we hardly remember our names,
but trust us—we feel still—thankful. In this now morning
after, this brutal wake-up silence, this downsidetippedup
outsidenowin we are deciphering, thank you thank you: if
only for these two words we all still easily re-call for now.
Listen—

Myrmecology

God I remember that time, the year I turned thirty: red ant ellipses, elegantly corseted, had frenzied around the magnolia spare room; their singular consciousness carefully transporting opal cargo loads between them. I didn't know why, but an almighty rage reared up and I sprayed the life out of the whole scattering colony with Baygon —Caribbean chemical warfare to fight your worst fear. I took off my rings, bleached up black ants unevolved mess from my bone-tiled floor; beige thick hand wiping out their existence with paisley-patterned cloth. I did not want them in my newly built house and knew no way of communicating, "go find yourselves another home".

For the next two days, I imagined hearing their stridulant fade-outs echoing against concrete wall, mixing with city music…then…the hurricane came and swept everything away. Now, I realise they had been leaving anyway, burdened by only what they needed to live. When I was a silent, translucent shadow of a bored brown single child, feeling stuffy in my cramped hot home, I would lose myself in the miniature commune of ants for hours; sticking my big head on stick-insect neck into their tiny country; studying their industrious formation marching to and fro across our pitted dusty wooden floor; their incessant slaving away, pulling, feelering, fetching, farming, foraging, feeding, birthing, burying, teaching, trailing, tidying, building…together. Once, unconsciously jealous of the power in their atomic package, I squashed one with my finger, gently, on its monstrously alien head, my small bright black bird eyes above them, invisible god unleashing hell, beaming and staying to watch the chaos. Then, it rained, for weeks. I remember too, me, ubiquitous tutting teenager, tortured by recurring nightmare: I was a black speck in a brave-new-all-ant world, enslaved by terracotta army who had colonised every mm of the planet. Single-file happy being instructed what to do, eternally, I thrashed legs and arms out of each dream, screeching; rough pale palms and soles rubbing cheap-puckered-cotton sheet and tearing at torn, tight, faded pyjamas. Now, here on this clear wet morning, my bone-tired fiftieth year, I sit in mountain-home quiet, still black hands on lap, air on fern-framed porch humid, and spy dead winged ants under the energy saving bulb; their spent male bodies laid out in a circle on the terracotta tiled floor. Funny, only last night I Googled about ants; thoughtfully birthed and nurtured to know their purpose and to play it out well, all the way to death; no fuss. How these seen scurrying figure eights are sterile or asexually cloning sisters. How the hidden-in-cave, long-life omnipotent queen, mother of all, ultimate baby-making machine, decides the genders created for prime colony living: every single androgynous egg, fertilised to daughter or left alone to be son. How they raise starved-weak, buck-princes, short-life drone sperm donors; that die for well groomed siren-princesses—spoilt single-minded nymphets—shimmering wings grown in place just long enough for the grand big-bang nuptial ball in the sky; then clipped, crowned, grounded for life, stomach-heavy with her very own creation kit. And all those efficiently-frigid die-hard-working proletariats; capable of birthing brothers for food. All one and one for All. The Hopi believe their ancestors were saved by Ant People descended in Egypt. I wonder if in time, formicultural knowledge can change anything for me, for you…for the greater good.

[9]

Mudras

The seventh day after the hurricane, we are all out
of water. Through new word-vine communication,
news flows of a source close by, & I go quick with
my empty plastic pail. A young man powered by
self motivation, stands sweating above a concrete

tank. He has been dipping & filling buckets since
early morning. His slender fingers blood-blistered.
The afternoon heat beats hard but he does not stop.
I wait my long-line turn, worked-hard hands resting,
clasped loosely on sunken belly. He fills. The mood

feels slightly heavy & muted & I sense a still sombre
undertow; most hands by sides & most heads down.
A dreadlocked woman holds fingers in front, shaped
to me like a powerful portal. A visibly agitated man
joins the line, hears a group chatting quietly ahead,

& points; yells loud loud: Dominicans should fill first,
before these Haitians. Commotion. Hands & voices
raise & raise. Recently I have been reading about the
power of hand gestures. I come from this rich cult-
ure of wild gesticulation & often, we fluently body

talk with a flowing, vociferous, vocality of hands.
The tired young man above the tank, stands steady
in his full raised height. He lifts straight up his middle
finger to the man; gives him cut-eye; snaps in Creole:
if you want water, shut up & wait your turn! We all nod.

Ode For Mum's Missing Roofing Screws
(Somewhere Still In The Universe)
After Kwame Dawes

There have been so many things to deal with, consider, after the hurricane, that we couldn't imagine…never would have wanted to.

Many say Maria was one hell of a storm but the happenings after we woke from her wake, were whole other all mighty storms to be living

through. Yes I know, we know, there is much to be grateful for, much we have still, in all the forms that life beautifully frames for us. But

now I am writing an ode to my mum's online ordered roofing screws; a small part of the huge tarpaulin puzzle of how we were going to get

her home covered again; how to re-assemble life to order as before. They were strong quality screws with hex heads. Cute metal caps &

neoprene washers would keep heavy rain from heavens out of holes screws pierced with pointed self drilling tips; letting water gush free

down galvanize into gutters, then ground. Not so much the missing of things, Kwame wrote in Ode to the Clothesline; & after the storm

we went back to living some old ordinary life ways that he spoke of. We walked slow, back and forth, across that strange taut rope lying

between horror and happiness, self reliance and assistance, being alone and in the spirit of community, holding on to…and letting go;

constantly; the joy—pain feelings of this un-covering redis-covering.
I know I have to let these missing roofing screws go. No-one can tell

me why they never made the sea passage from one land mass to this
one; just insured commodity they say, no matter—this time, I agree.

Horology - TimeXemiT(ion)
After Petőfi Sándor

Heart beats loud and fast. I've lost my cherished father's
watch he willed. A material thing perhaps, not worth emotion,
but my heart high-registers my carelessness all the same.

The watch band of large gold links, some removed to fit his tiny
wrist; the well scuffed worn face. This timepiece had survived Maria; no
Chronosphere but its quartz calibre powered a precise and steady pulse.

Unlike Me. I feel it will take years for things to run again
like clockwork. This time after the storm, I can't work out
exactly what month, day, hour my life so frantically inhabits.

In my teens, I remember how mad Dad was once; I gave a current love
a too-small ring of his—so easily. After we split, I asked him to return
it; but he had lost it at some point along our short but intimate timeline.

Now, I am reminded yet again—no thing is lost to the universe; not
even Dad's Timex watch or ring. I rewind the weeks and hours, retrace
movements and spend the day in search of another lost possession.

Listening for its distinct tick-tock emission, I hope it will turn up.
Something else I can't see or find for looking. For a second
another beat skips—what if it hasn't been misplaced—but taken?

Invoked

Santa Maria!   Human   you named me, teased   me out
          from the labyrinth of your   Dionysus   dreams
                    of a hurricane so   I am your   mother
intimately into   the white   look   now,   cyclops eye;   listen
          to the thundering   doom of my   clack-clack   cloven hooves.
                              In the   folds of my   fleeting   calm you will
                                        hear me   blow up the silence
                    with maddening   whispers   whispers.
                                        You   will:
try to make light   of my dark,   drink,   laugh out loud, try to   drown
me out   of your basement—I will   flood
you up the   streaming   stairs,   silent—sober;
          try to close   your heavy   shutters and   doors against
my whipping   my wailing—I will split   them like   coconuts;
          try to protect   your children,   swaddle them in   the crook
                              of your   fleshy arm—you
will stifle them all the way   to rigor mortis;

inside your mausoleum,   force you   to loath   loved ones
unburied bodies   on your bloody   marble kitchen table;
cling   onto the door of your   en-suite bathroom,
concrete sealed—in   two ferocious   shakes   a void,   unhinged;
you will shiver,   stare into
try to seek   shelter, a firm piece   of ground to   anchor
yourself—I will chew off each of your   seven covered chapters,   spittle them on   ribs
of flamboyant   trees and bury you   nude   in red-brown putrid mud.
Your rapacious black and white cat will saber-tooth your tongue   down to a stump,
claw out and   play   with your tonsils;
suck all grey-gloom night   on your   red-rich   your gold-chained pit bull will
rawboned marrow.
When I leave,   for all I know,   for all I   care,
you will seek   to solve   my riddle in   rubble,   ask why—
my mayhem will be a   lunatic's   mystery,
hurricane tied roofs   but   fluttering   over nailed tin on shack;
pressure popping
crushing crystal   caressing   calabash.

MY WINGS ARE NOT OF DOVES BUT BLACK AS BADB,
MY FEATHERS NOT LIGHT BUT DENSE AS TAR,
TALONS DIABOLICAL.
THERE WILL BE NO OLIVE-GREEN FOLIAGE LEFT
TO HIDE BEHIND PEACE
OF MIND.
I WILL TURN YOU LOOSE
I WILL TORNADO YOU OUT
OF YOUR RIGHT MIND.
I WILL LEAVE YOU LEAVE YOU
LEAVE YOU WITH NOTHING
WORTH SAVING—
THY. WILL.
BE. DONE.

Look up at this black tarpaulin sky: look into
this moon, these stars, your only guiding lights now.
—

In the miraculous morning, home intact, my daughter burst
open her heavy eyes and our
swelled shutters and doors—stared, pointed
at the flogged and naked, phantom trees;
brutally splintered limbs pointing all
over; black hollow knots in white tortured trunks mouthing—the horror.

There is a toothless guabancex-grinning woman
called Mad Maria, living under a bus shelter in a
now bare-bone village. She spins
out skeletal arms and cackles
when they still tease, call her name,
relentlessly.
I gifted my daughter the family name
Maria. She struck on her 13th birthday.
She sang hauntingly with eyes closed the
whole crashing night till dawn. I did not know
her words but metronomed with shak-shak
teeth and knocking knees.

Careful...
Maria Maria Maria—
collateral beauty—
bacchanal spirit—
exposed
we hope
we may not re-cover

H2.5AZ (Strong Ties, Galvanized)

They are building me a new roof since the old one went
with the wind—category 5 +. I have learnt a whole new
vocabulary—purlins, rafters, wall plates, hurricane ties.
It is chaos on top of chaos—the necessary brutal breaking
down to build back better, stronger—mitigate against future

blows they say will come more frequently—ferociously unpredictable.
I look up—sturdy wet new treated pine above my head, see the thicker
rafters—bird beaked—sitting tied down on edge of anchored plate.
They say you must have such cuts and ties to firmly lodge onto ledges—
the price to be secure—to be more—permanent; more knowledgeable?

Metamorphosis

Two years ago, just before
the hurricane, my husband
brought an animal into our
home. It found him, he said.

I never wanted a cat; never
trusted their claws or split eyes;
but had no other choice than to
accept his *but it's so cute* kitten.

It started with us a she, shy, but
came back from the vets male and
neutered; apparently a common
misidentification. So much has

changed since that time. Little
Kafka grown big, bold, litters our
home with body parts. Stalks.
Teases the lizards to death. Pounces.

Slyly swipes my bare feet as I pass.
Tonight the forest cockroaches have
come in full force. I have not yet learnt
their purpose. I lift high my grey furry
slipper and strike one down—mid flight.

Housing Revolution

Today, Sunday, my children are coming to have lunch with me here for the first time; here, in my new house. It was given to me by GoD after my old one was taken by the hurricane. i am so grateful, how can i be anything else? Of course things are different from my old village life;

but i'm thankful to be propelled forward, moving with times. The new apartment units are set close close together, in neat orderly rows, pale painted and with a tiny patch where i can grow some flowers. i have not yet grown accustomed, to not having my own back-yard garden,

but am grateful for this space to call my own again. So much has been lost, been shaken up, it feels good to be on stable ground once more. The ceiling shakes from the scurrying feet of the children upstairs and also, i have not got used to the thin wall separations; hearing my

neighbours' daily routine noises enter my sleep. We were close in our old village, often entering each other's homes to chat, eat, play dominoes and music; celebrate without formality. But we have been put together here from different places and it may take some time to build up a close-

knit community. It's a shame there is no river here close enough to go together; to wash our clothes or for the children to play around. GoD says a playground will come next and a school and hospital, just like i see on those American soap operas on my new smart cable TV. It was

the river that took all i had before, so i have to trust God truly works in ways i have yet to figure out. My children arrive late, they could not find which one was mine. The place echoes our cheerfulness. It feels like the old days. We join hands around the table; say grace; give God thanks.

My Sister & I Are Picking Mangoes

again in Mum's debris garden. Our tropical life has been
entropically re-coloured since the hurricane passed. She
came to help us & the hourglass days, turning over & over,
are often sublimely beautiful & surreal; brown pleasuring

to green/yellow/red; starred silver indigo, far too visible.
This beloved mango tree is recovery; she has us in awe
with her constant, almost embarrassing, fruit full giving.
I hold my husband's green fishing net: I know what it's

like to fall, bruise, split skin & expose flesh all the way
down to bone-white seed, so I pull down & catch; save
some mangoes from this fate. I imagine though the fruit
innately sense my nonsense; knowing there is no sin in

falling—grow, fall, feed ground/gut, grow again, repeat
infinitely. Brown hands pick up any spoilt grounded fruit,
toss them in the grown green gutter. Our aim? Deter flies
from hovering around; seeding worms into ripening fruit.

What Do I Know

Mr Elias John-Baptiste says they sent a biblical
hurricane so he could know God. Says God's eye
stayed above his house. Stared him out for 8 hours
just to make sure he was the right one. And he was.
Says God up lifted him high, boomed in air and brain,

look me, look me in this here whirlwind. I Mosiah
come with countless dead millions to help you out.
They do not know what you are capable of; they do
not know what you are thinking. I know you have
wrought well, wrought well; you are well-wrought and

ready to redeem. Mr John-Baptiste tells me all of this.
His family tells me that since the hurricane, he's lost
connection to what is real. His head is gone they say.
Elias lives only on Nood sea salt popcorn and spring
water. He smiles—smiles all the time; leaves hair dread-

ful long. There's nothing we can do for him but pray,
and give pills if he ever disturbs people too too much.
Mr Elias John-Baptiste tells me his mother lives in the
flooded wine cellar of his ruined house. She's a bright
black octopus. She feeds him a tentacle each day that

grows right back. He tells me our tallest mountain has
a flip-top lid and Cristóbal Colón lives deep deep inside.
Says Colón thinks our Zion is the New Jerusalem they need
and sees the twelve tribes of Israel all here in green Eden.
Mr Elias John-Baptiste asks me if I believe in anything

he says. I shrug. I say *Mr John-Baptiste maybe you're just not crazy about this world anymore; maybe you're mad mad mad about something. But what do I know?* He tells me he's the one God chose to heal the world. I say—*Aren't we all Mr John-Baptiste, aren't we all?*

Mr Elias John-Baptiste says he does not know where on good earth to start; has energetic answers now to every single question; exactly how to save the whole damn thing. Just not where to begin. I can only shrug again. *All I know is God did not start from anywhere.*

Hurricane PraXis (Xorcising Maria Xperience)

we are grateful to be alive   we are stunned to be still alive
we wade through dirty water   we mop water mop water mop water
we wipe up water from places we did not imagine water could go
we use every single towel/absorbent cloth in the house
we have no house left
we dig our way out break sealed doors/windows those that are still there
we string up washing lines   we string up more washing lines
we hang filthy things out to dry we hope we can wash them some day
we find dry spaces to sleep   make mattresses from what we can
we sleep in cars   we sleep in cupboards
we have bucket baths   we come up with creative ways to keep clean
we are always dirty
we go in search of family/neighbours/friends   they come in search of us
we go in search of clean water we carry water carry water carry water
we care for the injured the best we can   we bury our dead
we cannot find our dead   our dead are already buried
we try to stay positive   we laugh   we laugh hysterically
we cannot imagine ever laughing again
we chainsaw/cutlass chop trees   unblock roads   we walk for hours
we see stick trees mountains bare brown brown   no live animals
we see houses destroyed backyard gardens gone farms flattened flooded
we see a maze of electricity poles   wires wires wires
we see galvanize decorating bare branches
we imagine this is what a country looks like after a nuclear bomb
we see policemen with guns
we see people with bulging bags/supermarket trolleys/boxes on heads
we see them dragging boats we see them fight outside ransacked stores
we see mud mud mud   we smell sewage/all kinds of decomposition
we see people cleaning   clearing   sweeping out water
we see people rocking back and forth   people holding each other

[24]

we see people holding their heads   we do not see
we see parts of our communities we have never seen before
we see parts of our selves/others we have never seen before
we close our eyes   we do not look
we loot we have good good party with our loot   we do not loot
we are fearful of looters   we are angry with looters
we are angry with the police   we are angry with each other
we lock the doors and windows we still have
we hear nighttime noises we don't recognise
we don't hear tree frogs we don't hear crickets   we hear generators
we feel frightened   we take deep breaths   we sigh we sigh we sigh
we feel calm   we socialise   we have a good time
we have no utilities   we have no utility bills
we have leaks everywhere   we make bakes we drink cocoa tea
we run out of things to make bakes/cocoa tea
we wait for phone signals   we worry about those we cannot reach
we worry about those who will be worrying why they cannot reach us
we worry we will starve we will get sick we will go mad we will die
we worry about so much worrying
we listen constantly to the radio we listen to each other's experiences
we think some are funny   some are not
we cry together we cry in secret we pray together/alone we are silent
we hold each other   we are grateful we have each other
we are alone
we are endlessly cleaning clearing up   we salvage whatever we can
we overcome our fear of heights to patch up our roofs
we have no roof left to patch
we learn the best way to carry galvanize we learn all about tarpaulins
we learn which shred quick in the heat what noises they make in the wind
we get regular exercise our muscles grow strong we lose plenty weight
we get bruises/cuts all over we get infections headaches every part aches
we have no medication   no first aid kit
we have no shade from trees   we have no trees

we get sun burnt we get dark dark　　　we still love to watch the sunsets
we drink rum we drink gin and tonic we have no ice we have no water
we boil dirty water　　　we do not trust water sanitizing tablets
we are always hungry　　　　we never go hungry
we make a smoker for meat　　　we have freezers/cupboards full of food
we have no food　　　　　　we have no clean water
we create a tiny damp space to eat together we call it Maria restaurant
we joke about the creative menu　　　we stop thinking it is funny
we marvel at the places inside where we can see the stars
we learn to wear hats/rubber boots inside when it rains
we feel lucky to have a toilet inside　　　　we have no toilet
we time toilet breaks between helicopter passes　　　we laugh
we wonder where the helicopters come from
we wonder where they are going　　　who is leaving/coming
we devise clever ways to get rid of water inside our houses
we devise clever ways to stop water from getting inside our houses
we pray for rain　　　we pray for sun　　　we pray for rain to stop
we feel despair we feel depression　　　we feel desperation
we are paranoid　　　　　we panic
we feel vulnerable　　　we stay calm　　　　we feel safe
we go crazy　　　our pets go crazy　　　we get sick our pressure goes up
we get on with life/living
we hate the curfew　　　　　we are grateful for the curfew
we hate that we need to be grateful for the curfew
we obey the curfew　　　　we break curfew
we take what we desperately need　　　we take what we do not need
we take what we feel others are too mean to give
we take what we feel we will never have the means to have
we get our own back on others　　　others get their own back on us
we take what others have　　　we take what has been left unguarded
we take because we can take
we feel powerful for the first time　　　we do not feel powerful at all
we do not take　　　we give we give

we do not feel we have enough to give   we give anyway
we give when we do not know if/when we will receive
we are given we are given we are given   we share   we do not
we check on neighbours   neighbours check on us
we never check on our neighbours
we collect rain in old blue shipment barrels
we laugh when someone says it is water barrel economy
we worry this is no laughing matter   we are grateful to be alive
we burn books/furniture/clothes/possessions/our photo memories
we watch mould grow on walls   on ceilings   on furniture
we watch mildew eat our clothes/books/whatever is left
we burn more books/furniture/clothes/possessions/photos
we put more dirty things out to dry   they never seem to dry properly
we read books in the day that we never had time to read before
we tell each other stories at night that we never found time to before
we have no books to read   we cannot read
we compare this one to other hurricanes we experienced in the past
we have never experienced anything like this before
we are glad we do not have to go to work
we are angry we have to go to work
we no longer have a job to go to   we never had a job
we worry the children are missing school
we send the children away   we keep the children with us
we teach the children things they would not learn at school
we stay together   we stay alone
we leave together   we leave alone   we are left alone
we separate
we are forced to leave when we do not want to we can't wait to leave
we are forced to stay we have nowhere else to go no money to go
we stay when loved ones want us to leave
we leave when they want us to stay
we stay with each other and for each other
we leave each other and leave for each other

we have no idea what is the right thing to do
we feel guilty for leaving   we feel guilty for staying
we have no choice   we have choices
we are grateful to be alive
we will never come back   we never leave
we stay in our homes we stay in others' homes others stay in our homes
we stay in schools   we stay in churches
we stay in shelters that do not always feel safe   we are homeless
we go back to old ways of onepot cooking   old ways of washing
we learn new ways   we cope
we go to the river to bathe/wash clothes
we go to the river together to gather to cook to talk to laugh
we cannot go to the river   the river is too contaminated
we have no river to go to
we learn about solar lamps/headlamps/power packs
we learn about kinetic energy/ham radios
we use vehicles as stationary phone charging stations
we exchange food with each other
we long for garlic/onions/fresh seasoning/green fig/fresh fruit
we long for cold beer/ice
we need fresh food/toiletries/pampers/baby food
we need washing powder/disinfectant   we need so much
we long for more light at night
we have fuel we hope soon there will be bread we make our own bread
we even make our own fuel
we are thankful when rations start coming
we are thankful when water trucks come
we are given some rations we fight for rations someone takes our rations
we cannot go for rations we never get rations we don't want rations
we compare our rations with what others receive
we think the rations are great there is enough the items are needed
we think the rations are awful there is not enough the items are useless
we think so and so has better rations than us

we wonder why we are not getting any rations we hate needing rations
we long for fresh food   we feel ungrateful
we wonder why the PM does not like tinned sardines
we wonder if we should not like tinned sardines
we are grateful for the rations
we feel ungrateful for wanting different rations
we are grateful for the Haitians who sell provisions by the muddy road
we are not grateful for the Haitians we tell them to move somewhere else
we long for toilet paper
we long for a proper shower/bath/electricity/so many things
we are grateful for the shops that open up quick
we queue   we queue   we queue   we do not queue
we are outraged at the hiked up prices
we are told of increased overheads we are told of increased overheads
we stop going to the shops that treat us like criminals
we stop going to the shops because we have no money
we hate that some are behaving like criminals
we are not behaving like criminals
we are grateful phone companies work hard to get mobile data back quick
we suspect they worked so hard just to steal our money
we are mad   we are mad mad mad
we queue to complain   we queue to get our money back
we feel they are behaving like criminals
we feel low we feel they are low we feel powerless we feel disappointed
we are scared to use our phones
we worry our family overseas won't believe the money went quick quick
we are grateful to be alive
we learn about data/background apps/autorenew/out of plan data prices
we have to remember when data plan expiry dates and times are
we see birth re-birth buds birds green more green   we feel hopeful
we get used to seeing less   we get used to seeing more
we grow accustomed to what we see now what we don't see anymore
we get tired of the noise and smell of generators

we get frustrated we make noise noise noise get angry with each other
we meditate/sit in quiet contemplation/pray
we are grateful for all the help
we get angry with those overseas telling us what they think we should do
we get angry for getting angry
we are exhausted
we feel blessed we feel cursed we feel we are being taught a lesson
we thank god constantly for sparing our lives   we stop believing in god
we ask god why   we ask ourselves why
we stop asking questions
we become more faithful   we become more faith-less
we never had any faith
we queue outside the red cross zones   put our names on lists
we queue outside the red cross zones   put our names on lists
we stop putting names on lists   we stop queuing
we are so grateful for what we receive   we are ungrateful
we forget old quarrels   we start new fights
we do not quarrel   we do not fight
we cut each other's hair paint each other's nails
we dig holes in yards to bury rotten food/trash/toilet paper
we dig holes to bury all forms of waste   we bury anything we cannot burn
we put poison for roaches/rats   we scoop up dead roaches/rats
we make love
we sing out loud loud we beat our drums play our jing ping instruments
we play our shakshaks   we cannot
we lose our voices   we cannot speak   we do not want to speak
we are thankful we had paid for insurance
we are suspicious of insurance companies   we have no insurance
we submit insurance claims   we wait   they reject our figures
we submit again   we wait
we are constantly chasing   we hear nothing
we feel low   we feel they are low
we feel powerless   we feel angry   we feel disappointed

we are grateful to be alive
we feel forced to misbehave to be heard / to be taken seriously
we wait
we feel powerless   we feel devastated   we feel hopeless
we are hopeful   we are grateful to be alive
we are grateful plenty relatives / friends / strangers here / overseas send aid
we are grateful plenty people send money   send   send
we see so many people from other countries come to help
we see so many charities come to help
we see so many come to help so many come to help to help so many help
we give thanks   we are grateful
we hope one day we can help ourselves more
we hope one day we can go overseas somewhere to help others
we have lost so much   we have not lost anything
we do not know where to start when asked what we need
we do not know when to stop when asked what we need
we do not get asked what we need   we don't need anything
we need everything   we are grateful for what we have left
we have nothing left
we never imagined living through a time so hard
we imagine it could be much harder
we see positive things we will never forget
we see negative things we will never forget
we are in awe of the depth of compassion we experience
we are in awe of the lack of compassion we experience
we worry we are not being resilient enough not Dominica Strong enough
we are strong we are resourceful we are creative / courageous / coping
we are breaking
we help ourselves we can help ourselves more we do what we can
we have each other   we have family   we have community
we care about each other   we care about our country
we care about ourselves   we do not care enough
we grieve   we do not grieve enough

we may never stop grieving   we will never stop caring
we have always been resilient   we wish we did not always have to be
we feel proud of ourselves/each other   we feel ashamed
we feel tired   we feel energised
we feel scared   we feel courageous
we feel hopeful   we feel hopeless
we feel empowered   we feel powerless
we feel abandoned   we feel loved
we feel strong   we feel exhausted
we feel traumatised   we feel trapped   we have never felt so free
we feel so many conflicting emotions
we get tired of feeling   feeling   feeling
we get tired of needing   needing   needing
we are tired still   feel still   need still   recovering still
…
we think about it all the time   we don't want to think about it at all
we may never be the same   we may never see things the same way
things will never be the same again
…
I have started learnin
                       growin from this xperience
I have started seein
                       differently   seein what I still have faith in
I have started doin
                       what I be-live
I have started re-buildin
                       character   home   community
I have
      been left with
            less   left with   more   life to taste more to test
I have
      been left
            wholly changed   unchanged